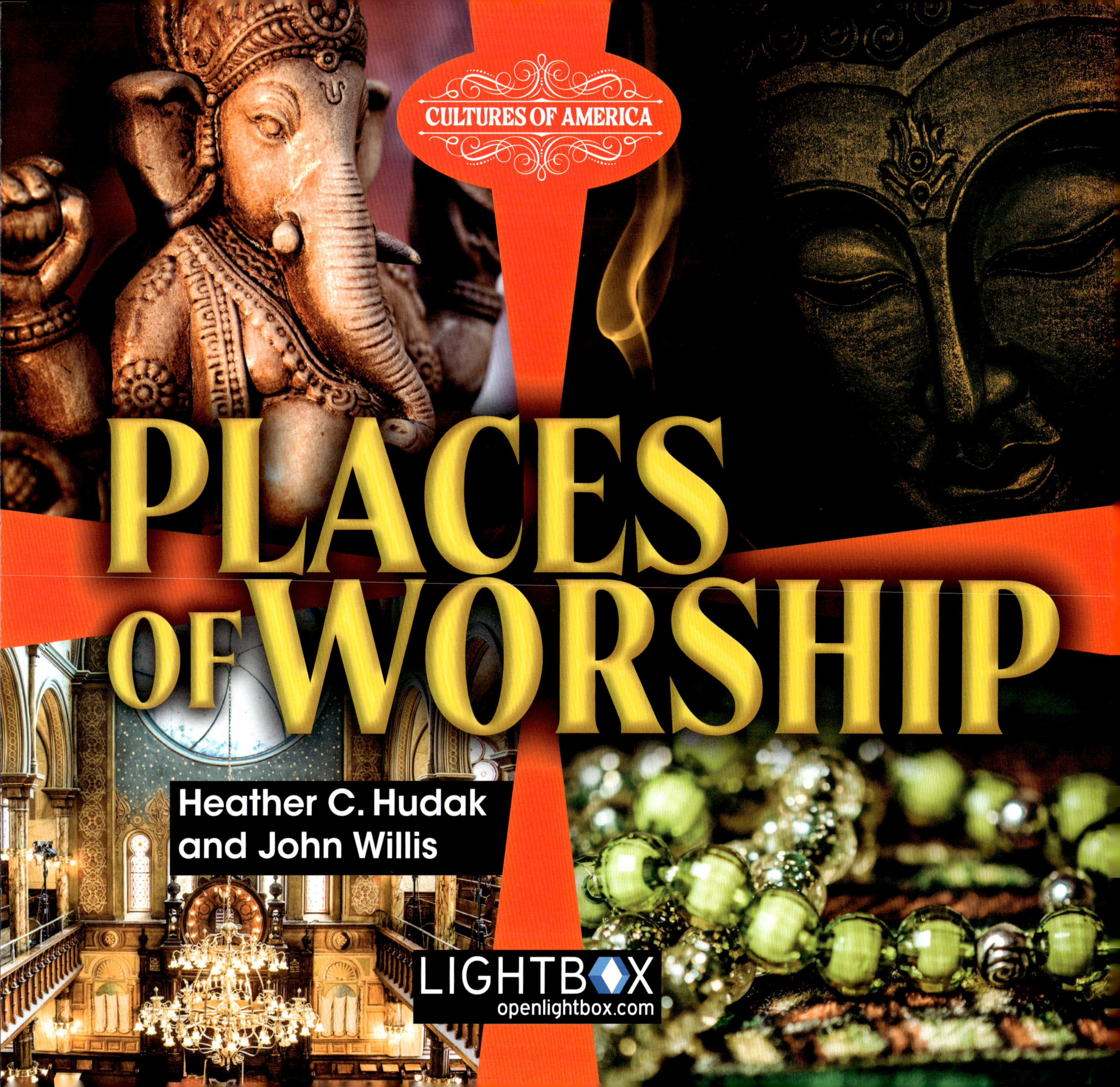
CULTURES OF AMERICA
PLACES OF WORSHIP
Heather C. Hudak
and John Willis
LIGHTBOX
openlightbox.com

LIGHTBOX

Go to **www.openlightbox.com** and enter this book's unique code.

ACCESS CODE

LBXR8725

Lightbox is an all-inclusive digital solution for the teaching and learning of curriculum topics in an original, groundbreaking way. Lightbox is based on National Curriculum Standards.

OPTIMIZED FOR

- ✓ TABLETS
- ✓ WHITEBOARDS
- ✓ COMPUTERS
- ✓ AND MUCH MORE!

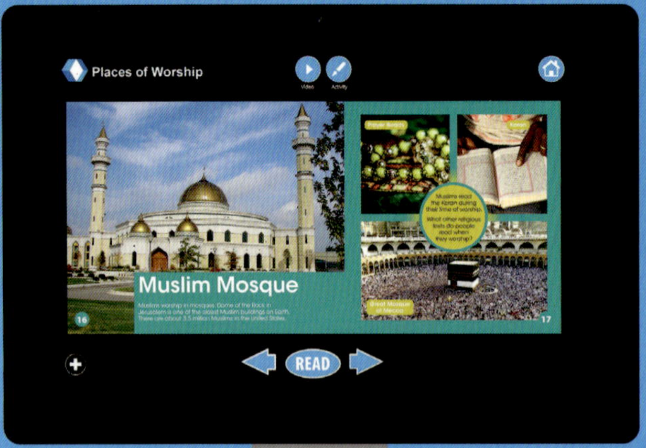

STANDARD FEATURES OF LIGHTBOX

- **AUDIO** High-quality narration using text-to-speech system
- **VIDEOS** Embedded high-definition video clips
- **ACTIVITIES** Printable PDFs that can be emailed and graded
- **WEBLINKS** Curated links to external, child-safe resources
- **SLIDESHOWS** Pictorial overviews of key concepts
- **INTERACTIVE MAPS** Interactive maps and aerial satellite imagery
- **QUIZZES** Ten multiple choice questions that are automatically graded and emailed for teacher assessment
- **KEY WORDS** Matching key concepts to their definitions

SUPPLEMENTARY RESOURCES

- **SHARE** Share titles within your Learning Management System (LMS) or Library Circulation System
- **CURRICULUM** Find national and state curriculum correlations
- **CITATION** Create bibliographical references following the Chicago Manual of Style

VIDEOS

WEBLINKS

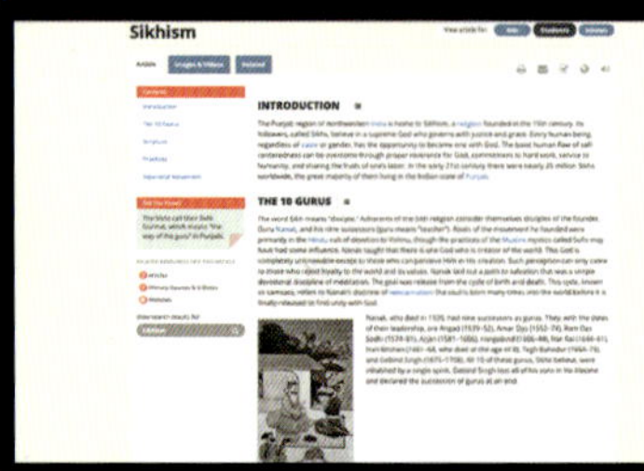

SLIDESHOWS

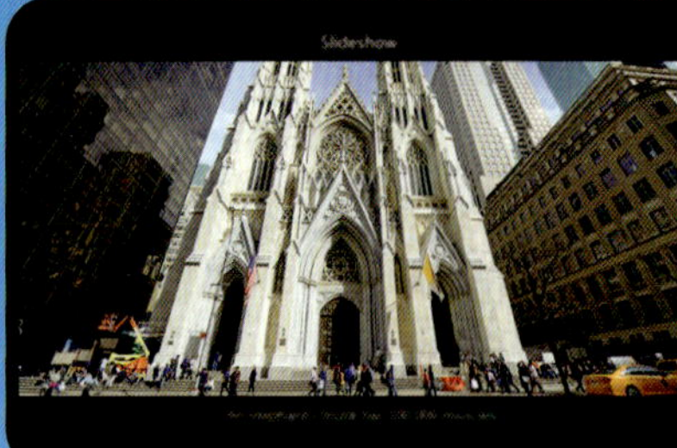

QUIZZES

This title is part of our Lightbox digital subscription

Lightbox Grades K–5 Subscription
ISBN 978-1-5105-5712-3

Access hundreds of Lightbox titles with our digital subscription. Sign up for a **FREE** subscription trial at **www.openlightbox.com/trial**

PLACES OF WORSHIP

CONTENTS

Catholic Church

Catholics are a Christian group. Like other Christian groups, they follow the teachings of Jesus Christ. Catholics worship in churches. More than 20 percent of all Americans are Catholic.

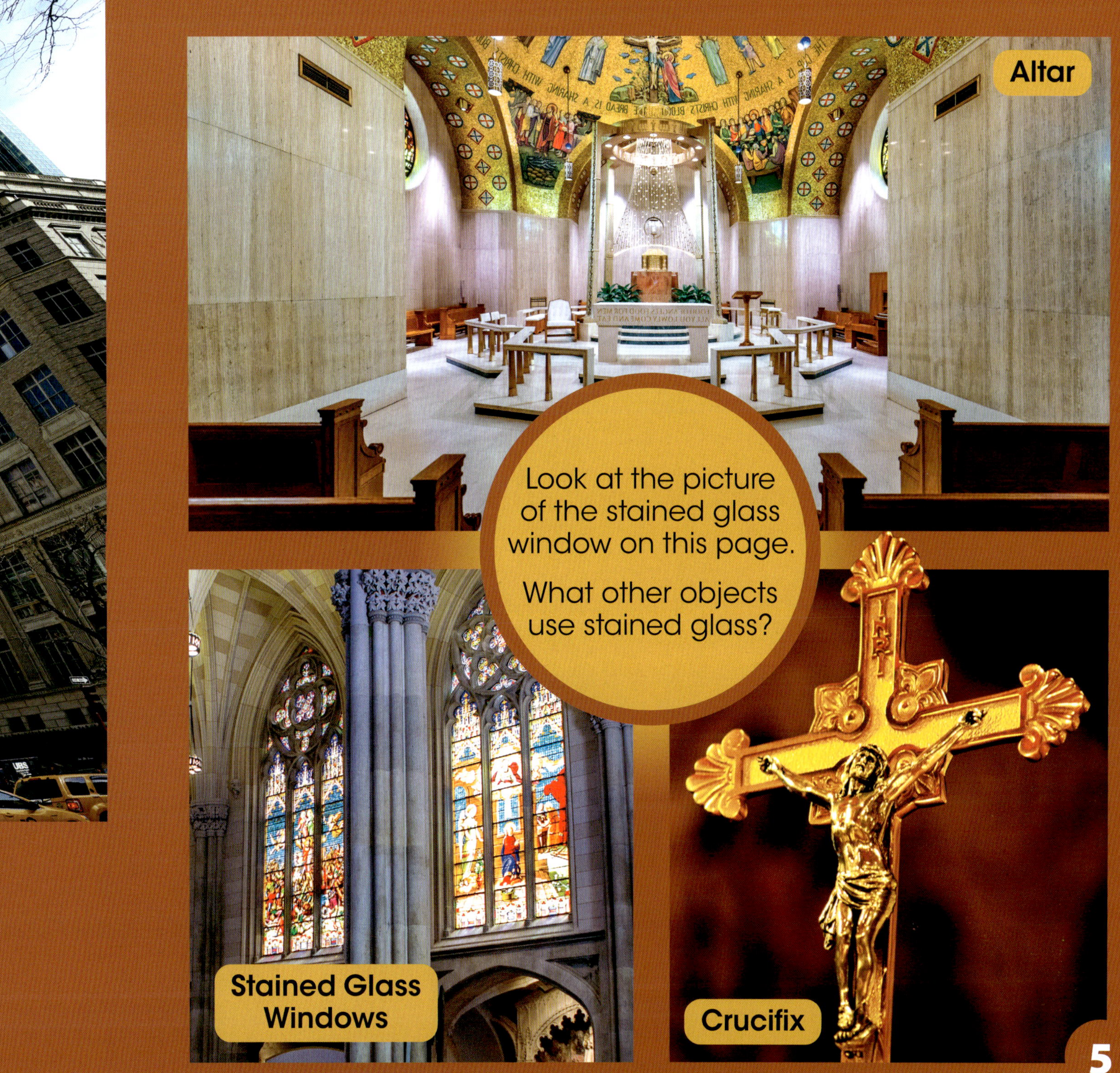

Look at the picture of the stained glass window on this page.

What other objects use stained glass?

Buddhist Temple

Many people follow the teachings of Buddha. They worship at a temple. A picture or statue of Buddha is inside the temple. Many Buddhists have a shrine at home. It may include a statue of Buddha, candles, and incense.

Many Buddhist temples have statues.

What types of statues are found in other places of worship?

Sikh Gurdwara

Sikhs worship in places called gurdwaras. A gurdwara is thought of as the doorway to a guru's house. A guru is a religious guide. People must take off their shoes before they enter a gurdwara. They must also wash their hands and cover their head.

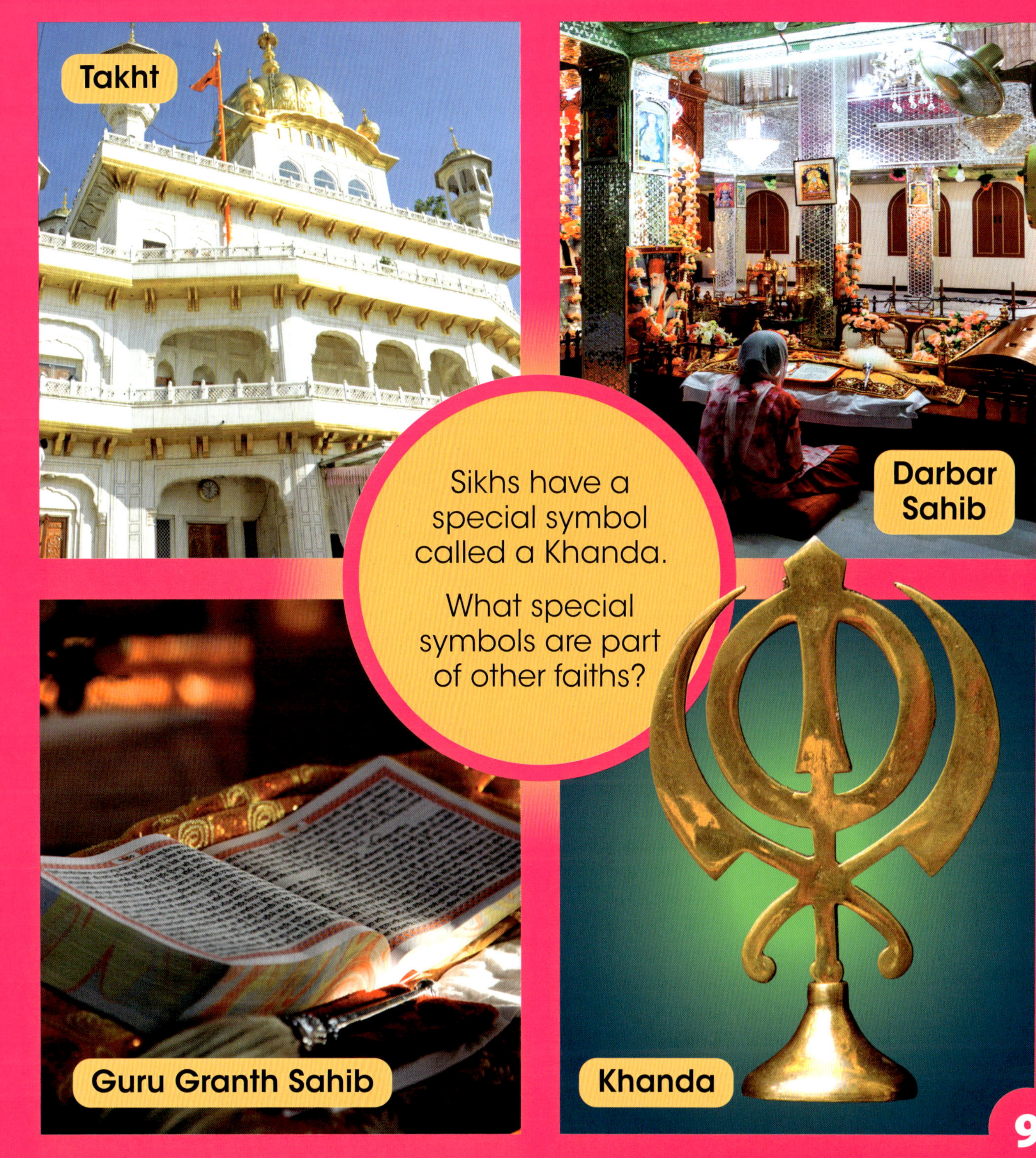

Sikhs have a special symbol called a Khanda.

What special symbols are part of other faiths?

Lakota Sweat Lodge

Across the United States, different Native American groups, including the Lakota, practice their beliefs in different ways. One of the most important Lakota ceremonies is the *Inipi*, or sweat lodge. During an Inipi ceremony, heated rocks are used to create steam while people pray and sing.

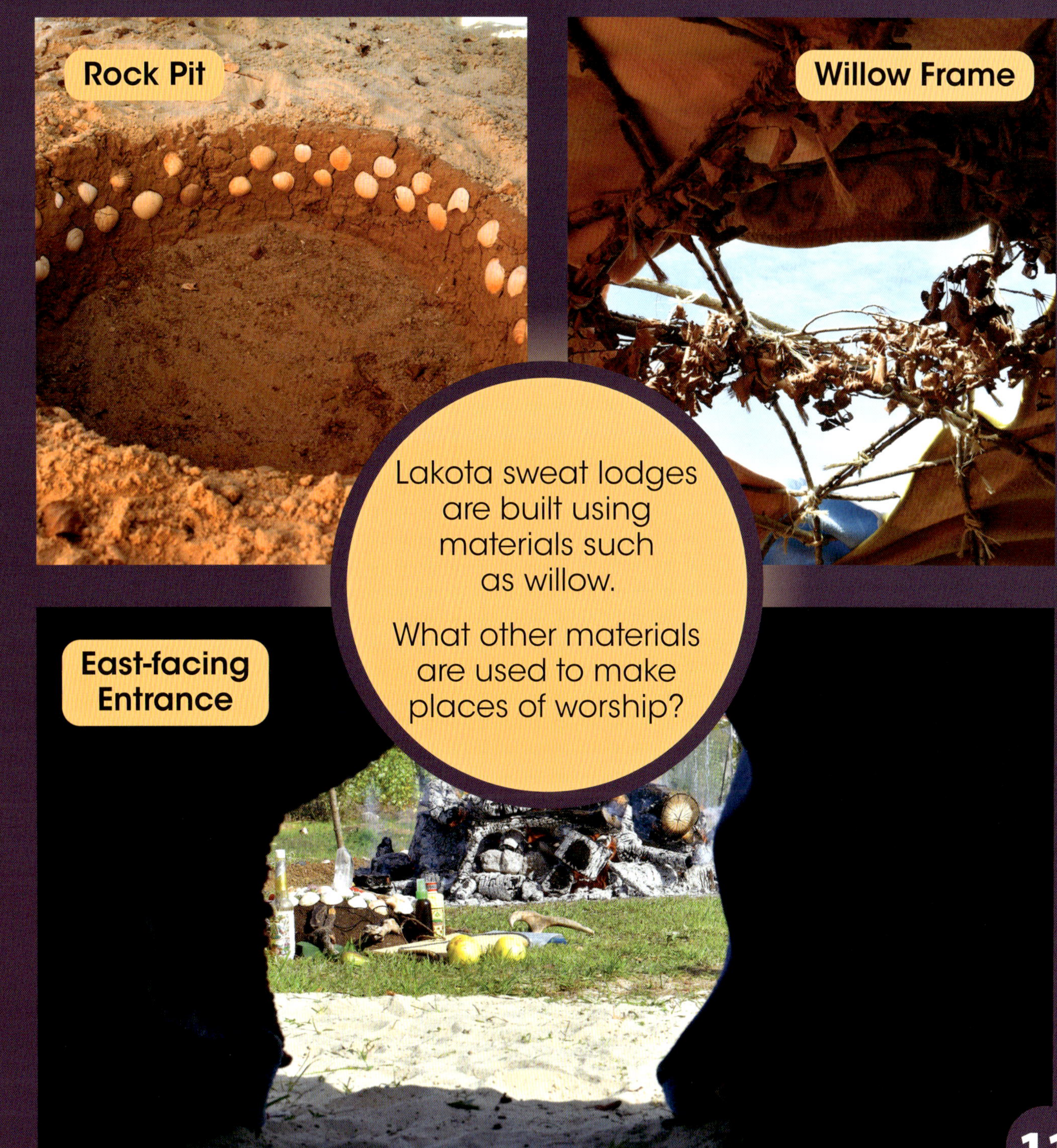

Lakota sweat lodges are built using materials such as willow.

What other materials are used to make places of worship?

Jewish Synagogue

The Jewish religion centers around the family, community, home, and synagogue. The Jewish holy day is called Shabbat. Shabbat begins at sundown on Friday evening. It ends after sundown on Saturday evening.

Menorah

Torah

The candles on a menorah are lit during Hanukkah.

What other faiths use candles during worship?

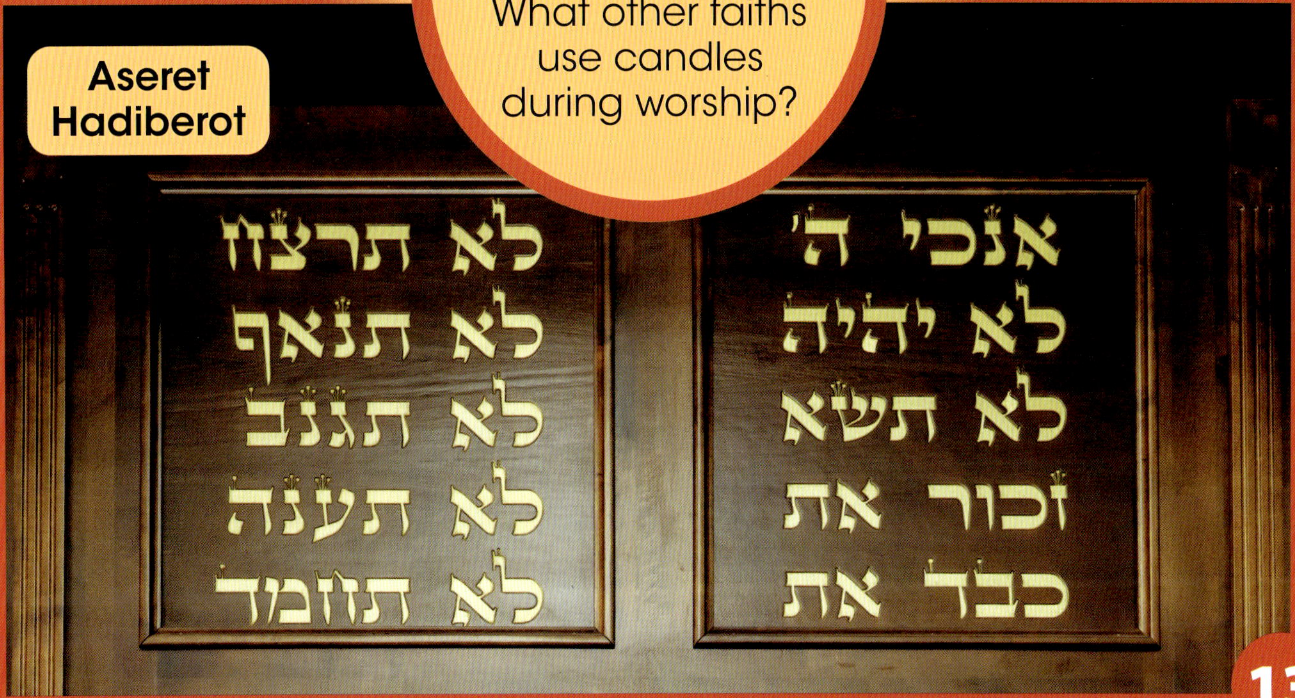

Aseret Hadiberot

אנכי ה'
לא יהיה
לא תשא
זכור את
כבד את

לא תרצח
לא תנאף
לא תגנב
לא תענה
לא תחמד

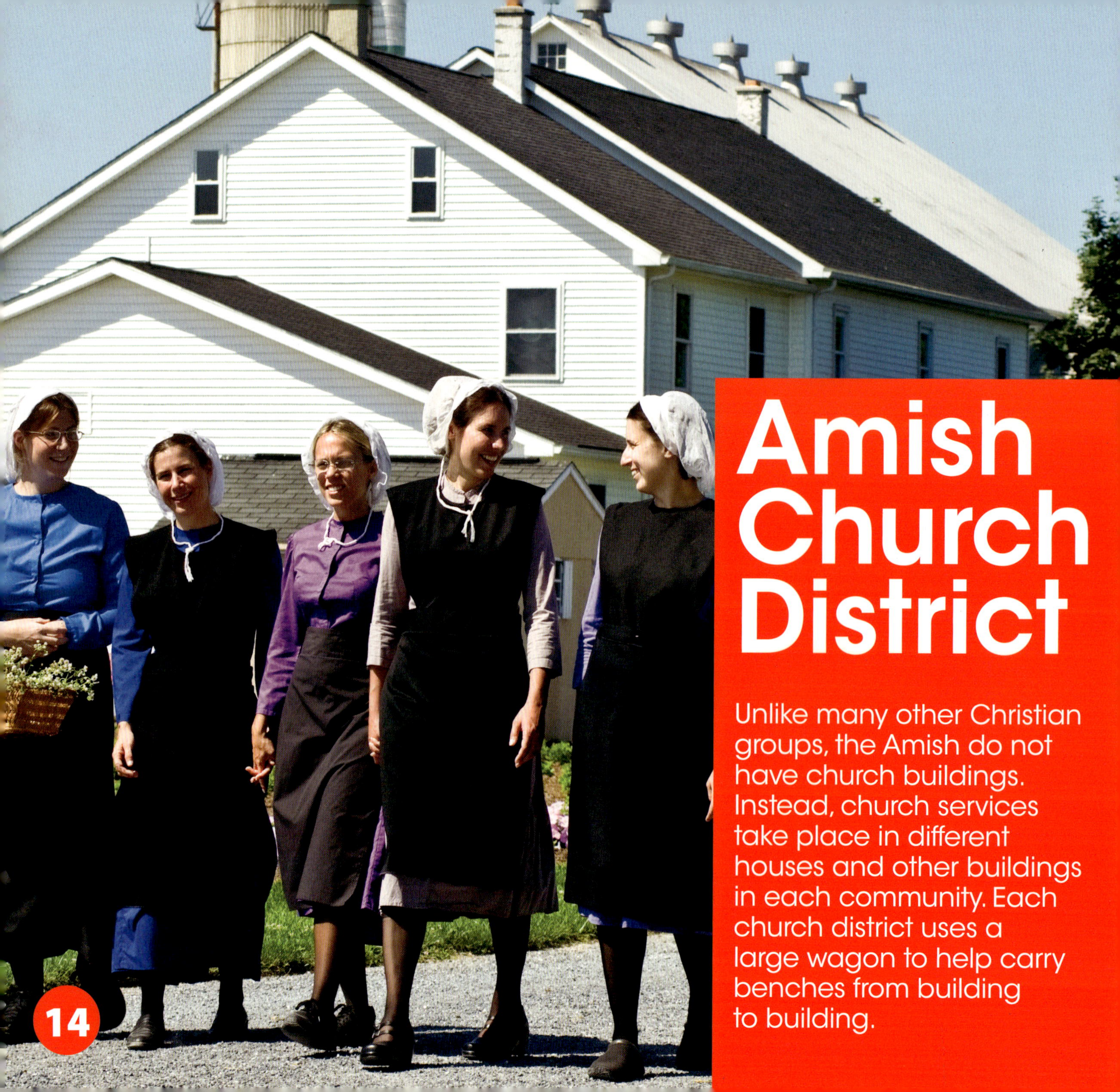

Amish Church District

Unlike many other Christian groups, the Amish do not have church buildings. Instead, church services take place in different houses and other buildings in each community. Each church district uses a large wagon to help carry benches from building to building.

Wagons

Bible

The Amish perform church services in their homes.

Where else do people worship?

Homes

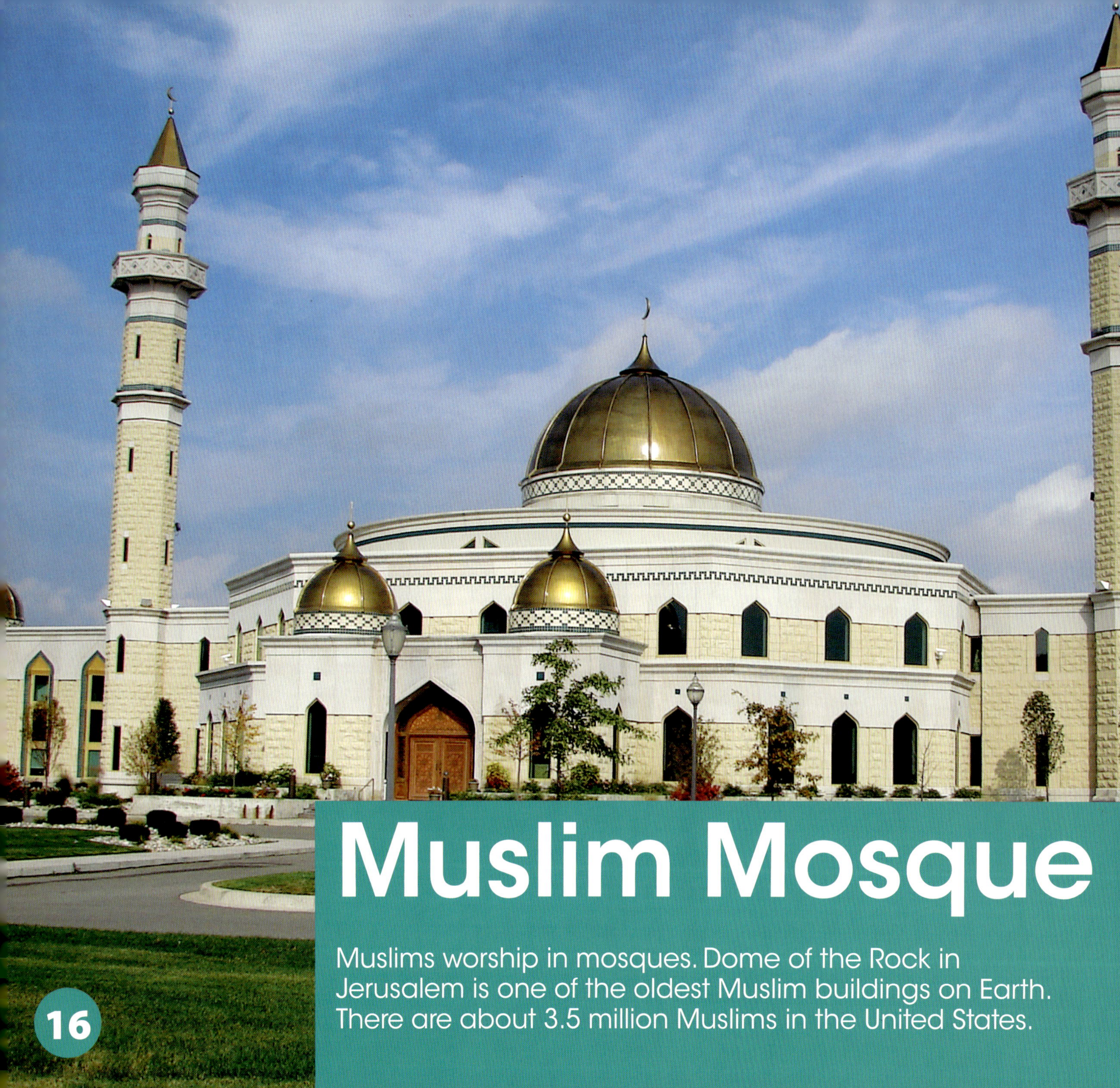

Muslim Mosque

Muslims worship in mosques. Dome of the Rock in Jerusalem is one of the oldest Muslim buildings on Earth. There are about 3.5 million Muslims in the United States.

Muslims read the Koran during their time of worship.

What other religious texts do people read when they worship?

Hindu Temple

Many Americans from India and Sri Lanka are Hindu. They worship in temples. The BAPS Shri Swaminarayan Mandir in Robbinsville, New Jersey, is the largest Hindu temples in the United States.

Hindus prepare special places, called shrines, to worship.

Where do people worship other than shrines?

Baptist Church

Baptists have members all over the United States. They are one of many Protestant Christian groups. All Baptists are baptized by having their whole body placed underwater.

Baptists are baptized using water.

How might other religious groups use water?

Matching Activity

You have learned about many places of worship in the United States.

Match the name of each place below to the correct picture.

Jewish Synagogue	Sikh Gurdwara	Hindu Temple
Buddhist Temple	Baptist Church	Catholic Church
Muslim Mosque	Lakota Sweat Lodge	Amish Church District

KEY WORDS

Research has shown that as much as 65 percent of all written material published in English is made up of 300 words. These 300 words cannot be taught using pictures or learned by sounding them out. They must be recognized by sight. This book contains 79 common sight words to help young readers improve their reading fluency and comprehension. This book also teaches young readers several important content words, such as proper nouns. These words are paired with pictures to aid in learning and improve understanding.

Page	Sight Words First Appearance
4	a, all, Americans, are, group, in, like, more, of, other, than, the, they
5	at, look, on, page, picture, this, what
6	and, have, home, is, it, many, may, or, people
7	found, places
8	also, as, before, hands, head, house, must, off, take, their, thought, to
9	part
10	an, different, important, most, one, states, used, ways, while
11	make, such
12	after, around, day, ends, family
14	carry, do, each, from, help, large, not
15	where
16	about, Earth, there
17	read, time, when
20	by, over
21	how, might, water

Page	Content Words First Appearance
4	Catholics, church, Jesus Christ, teachings
5	altar, crucifix, objects, stained glass windows
6	Buddha, Buddhists, candles, incense, shrine, statue, temple
7	bell
8	doorway, guide, Gurdwara, guru, shoes, Sikhs
9	Darbar Sahib, Guru Granth Sahib, Khanda, symbol, Takht
10	ceremony, Lakota, rocks, steam, sweat lodge, United States
11	entrance, frame, materials, pit, willow
12	community, religion, Shabbat, synagogue
13	Aseret Hadiberot, Hanukkah, menorah, Torah
14	benches, buildings, district, services, wagon
15	Bible
16	Dome of the Rock, Jerusalem, mosque, Muslims
17	Great Mosque at Mecca, Koran, prayer beads, texts
18	BAPS Shri Swaminarayan Mandir, Hindu, India, New Jersey, Robbinsville, Sri Lanka
19	deities, diya
20	Baptists, members
21	cross

Published by Lightbox Learning
276 5th Avenue, Suite 704 #917
New York, NY 10001
Website: www.openlightbox.com

Library of Congress Control Number available upon request.

ISBN 978-1-5105-6003-1 (hardcover)
ISBN 978-1-5105-6004-8 (multi-user eBook)

Printed in Guangzhou, China
1 2 3 4 5 6 7 8 9 0 25 24 23 22 21

092021
110820

Designer: Ana María Vidal Project Coordinator: John Willis

Every reasonable effort has been made to trace ownership and to obtain permission to reprint copyright material. The publisher would be pleased to have any errors or omissions brought to its attention so that they may be corrected in subsequent printings. The publisher acknowledges Alamy, Getty Images, and Shutterstock as the primary image suppliers for this title.